My Country
Brazil

Annabel Savery

A⁺

Smart Apple Media

Published by Smart Apple Media
P.O. Box 3263, Mankato, Minnesota 56002
www.blackrabbitbooks.com

Published by arrangement with the Watts Publishing
Group LTD, London.

Library of Congress Cataloging-in-Publication Data

Savery, Annabel. Brazil / Annabel Savery.
p. cm. — (My country)
Summary: "Introduces readers to Natalia, who lives in
Brazil. Describes Brazil's landscape, weather, family life,
food, and national holidays. Includes a fast facts page
on Brazil's population, geography, and culture"
—Provided by publisher.
Includes bibliographical references and index.
ISBN 978-1-59920-902-9 (library binding)
1. Brazil—Juvenile literature. I. Title.
F2508.5.S285 2015
981—dc23
              2012024743

Series Editor: Paul Rockett
Series Designer: Paul Cherrill for Basement68
Picture Researcher: Diana Morris

Every attempt has been made to clear copyright. Should
there be any inadvertent omission please apply to the
publisher for rectification.

Picture credits: Atlaspix/Shutterstock: 4b; crazycoat/
istockphoto: 20; Nicholas DeVore/Photoshot: front cover
l, 12; Julio Etchart/Alamy:17; Fabio Fersa/Shutterstock: 8;
David R Frazier/Alamy: 14; Front Page/Shutterstock: 5;
Ricardo Funari/Brazil Photos/Alamy: 16; Robert Harding
World Imagery/Getty Images: 15; Hemis/Alamy: front cover
c, 4t, 7 inset, 11 inset, 14 inset, 18 inset, 22; Christopher
Kolaczan/Shutterstock: front cover r, 13; Johnny Lye/
Shutterstock: 7; Edward Marques-Mortimer/Dreamstime:
18; Paura/Dreamstime: 9; Picture Alliance/Photoshot: 10;
Eduardo Rivero/Shutterstock: 2, 21; Celso Sellmer/www.
flickr.com/photos/celsosellmer <http://www.flickr.com/
photos/celsosellmer> : 19; Spectral-Design/Shutterstock:
3, 6; Janine Weidel Photography/Alamy: 1, 11.

Printed in Stevens Point, Wisconsin at Worzalla
PO 1654
4-2014

9 8 7 6 5 4 3 2 1

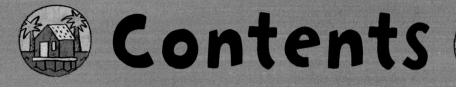 Contents

All words in **bold**
appear in the
glossary on page 23.

 Brazil in the World

My name is Natalia and I come from Brazil.

Brazil is in the **continent** of South America. It is the biggest country in South America and the fifth largest in the world.

Brasília

Rio de Janeiro
São Paulo

Brazil's place in the world.

4

I live in Brazil's **capital** city, Brasília. Brasília is a new city. Other cities, such as São Paulo and Rio de Janeiro, are much bigger and much older.

Brasília was built as a new capital city in 1960.

Brazil's Landscape

Brazil has more than 4,350 miles (7,000 km) of coastline.

Brazil is a huge country and has many different types of land. In the south, there are high mountains and thick forests. In eastern Brazil, there is a long coastline with lots of beaches.

The enormous Amazon River is in northern Brazil.

Around the Amazon River there are wet swamplands and tropical rain forests. The weather here is hot and **humid**.

Millions of animals, insects, and plants live and grow in the rainforest.

My favorite animal, the pink river dolphin, lives in the Amazon River. What's your favorite animal?

The Weather in Brazil

Northern Brazil is near the **equator**. This means it is hot all year round. In the northeast there is not much rain, so there are often **droughts**.

The land gets very dry when it is hot and there is little rain.

In the south, the weather changes throughout the year. It is coldest between May and September.

The warmer season is between October and April. This is also when it rains the most.

High up in the mountains it can get very cold, especially at night.

At Home with My Family

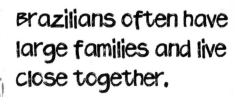

At home, I live with my mom, my dad, and my big brother Pedro.

Brazilians often have large families and live close together.

On weekends and vacations, we visit our family in Rio de Janeiro and play games on the beach.

Rio de Janeiro is the second biggest city in Brazil. The biggest city is São Paulo.

Soccer is the most popular sport in Brazil.

I like playing soccer with my cousins. What is your favorite sport?

People Who Live in Brazil

Over time, many different people have come to live in Brazil. This means that Brazilian people today have **ancestors** from all over the world.

Brazilian people have European, African, and Amerindian roots.

Most people live in the south where there are big cities. Toward the edge of the cities there are large **shanty towns**.

Other people live in the country, where they work on farms and raise animals.

Houses in the shanty towns are poorly built and overcrowded.

What We Eat

Most meals include meat, rice, and vegetables.

The best thing about living in Brazil is the food. My mom is a great cook, and at home we all eat together.

My favorite food is steak with black beans. What's yours?

Street stalls sell food that
is ready to eat, such as *pasteles*.
These are pastry envelopes
with beef in the middle.

Brazil's national dish is
feijoada completa, a meat
stew with beans.

*Feijoada completa
is served with rice
and slices of
orange.*

15

Going to School

Children in Brazil go to school from ages 7 to 14. I am still at primary school.

During the week I go to school for four hours every day, from seven in the morning until lunchtime.

My friends at school are studying hard.

Some children from poorer families do not go to school. They stay at home to help their parents or go out to earn money.

This girl is making traditional crafts to sell.

Festivals and Celebrations

Carnival is a huge celebration. It happens in February, before **Lent,** and lasts for five days.

In Rio de Janeiro, streets are filled with music, dancing and people in costumes.

Most people in Brazil are Roman Catholics. This means that we celebrate lots of religious holidays. In November, we celebrate the Day of the Dead, when we remember people who have died.

People celebrate the Day of the Dead by lighting candles and taking flowers to relatives' graves.

Things to See

There are many amazing things to see in Brazil. Above Rio de Janeiro there is a big hill called Corcovado Peak. On top of this is an enormous statue of Christ the Redeemer.

The Christ the Redeemer statue is 125 feet (38 m) tall!

For our last vacation we went to visit the Iguaçu Falls. This is a huge waterfall in southern Brazil on the border with Argentina.

There are actually 270 separate falls. The drop is 197 feet (60 m) high!

Here are some facts about my country!

Fast Facts about Brazil

Capital city = Brasília

Population = 203,429,773

Currency = the real (R$)

Area = 3,287,612 sq. mi.
(8,514,877 km^2)

Language = Portuguese

National holiday = September 7 (Independence Day)

Main religion = Christian

Longest river = The Amazon, 3,977 miles (6,400 km)

Highest mountain = Pico da Neblina, 9,823 feet (2,994 m)

Glossary

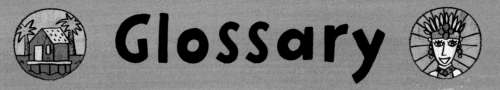

ancestor a person you are related to who lived a long time ago

capital the most important city in a country

continent a very large area of land—there are seven on Earth

drought a long period of time when there is little or no rain

equator an invisible line that runs around the center of the globe

humid having a lot of water vapor in the air

Lent the 40 days before Easter that Christians observe by fasting

shanty town a very poor area of a town that has low quality housing

Further Information

Websites

http://kids.nationalgeographic.com/kids/places/find/brazil/

http://www.brazilintheschool.org/p/brazil-for-kids.html

Books

Franchino, Vicky. *Brazil (It's Cool to Learn about Countries).* Cherry Lake, 2011

Morrison, Marion. *Brazil (Countries Around the World).* Heinemann, 2012

Parker, Ed. *Discover Brazil (Discover Countries).* PowerKids Press, 2010

Savery, Annabel. *Brazil (Been There).* Smart Apple Media, 2012

Index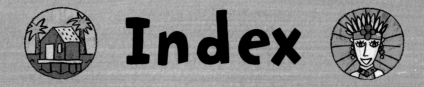